Furry Toes and All

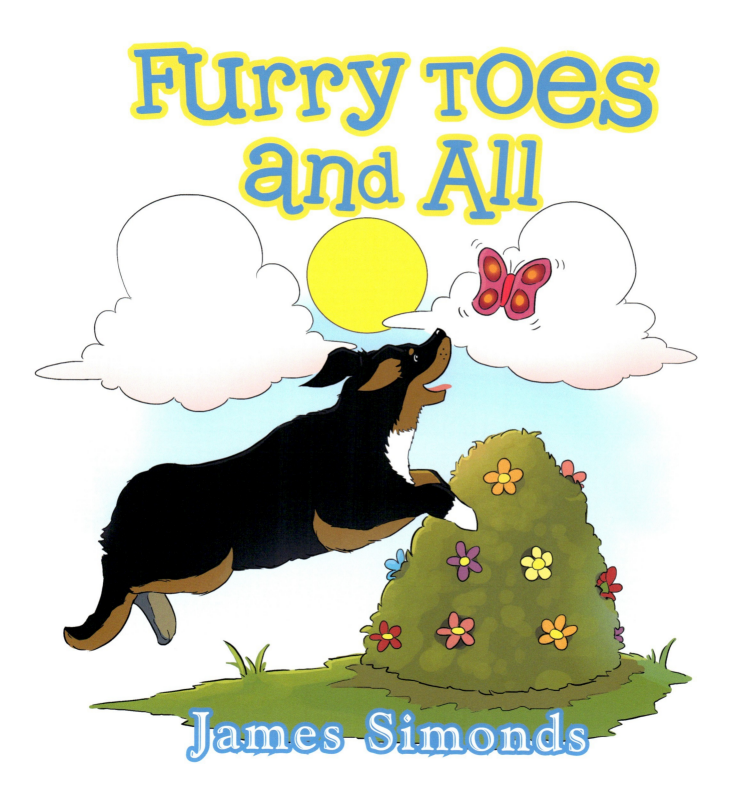

James Simonds

To order additional copies of this book, contact:
Xlibris
1-888-795-4274
www.Xlibris.com
Orders@Xlibris.com

Furry Toes
and All

Furry Toes and All

I'm just a little dog
Today I'm 5 years old
My fur is black just like my nose
I'm still a pup I'm told

I have four legs, no tail to wag
And I am almost small
I'll tell my life through my brown eyes
With furry toes and all

The first thing I remember
When I opened eyes to see
Were two brown eyes of wonder
Looking down at me

I knew you were my mother
Do you know how I knew?
Because you never left my side
Kept me warm the whole day through

You made me feel so safe and calm
When I was close to you
You fed me milk and gave me love
You're a girl, I am one too

The first thing I learned was this
I had to share with others
Because your love was meant for all
And I had two bigger brothers

I didn't like them much at first
They nipped and laid on me
But I soon learned to share with them
Because I was really one of three

The first few weeks we ate and grew
We rarely left Mom's side
We shared her love, her warm soft fur
Until 6 eyes opened wide

While my eyes grew brighter
I watched my brothers grow
Fat tummies, whimpers stronger
Mine did the same you know

I still have a tummy
I have furry toes and all
And I still have big brown eyes
But I'm not nearly as small

Eventually we wandered
My two brothers and I
Mom let us discover
Both bugs and butterflies

Not far away at first
She was always close you see
Always keeping us together
It's best to see as three

We learned our voice
At first a yelp
Of course we copied her
Once a yelp, and now a bark and I became myself

What am I you're asking?
All black with brown and white
The first I learned I was a pup
And I seemed to grow at night

I know I am a girl pup
My brothers both are boys
We're different in so many ways
But we still share our toys

I mentioned bugs and butterflies
We all love to chase and nip
We just kept trying, never gave up
Especially me so here's a tip

Your legs are short it's not far down
No matter if you stumble
Just get back up on your own two feet
It's not too far to tumble

If you're like me, your Mom will be there
To catch you by the scruff
To set you down and try again
To stop trying is giving up

So at first we had a pen to romp
And we were safe we three
Everything seemed big back then
But we were small and free

We ran, we chased, and we wrestled
We grew, we learned, we loved
In that small space that once was home
A fence with the sky above

The fence kept us safe from going far
We all wanted from her to stray
But Mom was there with a watchful eye
And never far away

As our home grew bigger
With much more space for us to run
We ran, we jumped, we tumbled
Chasing butterflies flies was fun

Then one day it happened
A new set of feet to see
It was the first time I looked up
And you were staring down at me

13

You giggled, I licked, and you laughed
Do you remember that?
I still remember your touch on my ears
And I smiled at your silly hat

I couldn't get close enough
To be near you, I wanted out
So I scratched and nuzzled
For more of you no doubt

My non-existent tail wagged
My brothers knocked me down
And you scolded them, not me
A frown tuned upside down

My paws atop the fence
Your beautiful face in mine
Your squeals and laughter rises
So full of warm sunshine

I have made a new friend
It's very clear to me
You didn't leave my side
And with me close to you, together we will be

So do you think that pups have feelings?
I can tell you that we do
I didn't want to say good bye
I knew I was meant for you

So a bath I had and papers signed
I didn't like that part
But I tolerated it for you
We had each other's heart

Then a collar, what is this
Thing around my neck
It is not a part of me
Are we going on a trek?

Then a hooky thing, and a gentle tug
My legs go out from under
I could dust the floor this way
Should I do the dusting I wonder?

17

But I'm a smart little thing you know
I seem to learn real fast
I am supposed to follow
Our togetherness will last

I'm really all smell and sense
The car was smell anew
But I was small, you held me close
I got the smell of you

I think I probably shook
New senses make me do that
But I was never frightened
Because I liked your silly hat

New sounds, new touches, new smells
My senses all a jangle
So I snuggle up real close to you
My fur your fingers entangle

A few things that I've learned so far
And you will learn them too
Butter flies, bees buzz
And strangely, people wear shoes

Oh, and one more thing
I'm no longer a pup
I have a name
I'm Maisey now, what's up!

Is this my new home I wonder?
This thing that seems so fast
I hope it is because we fly inside
And I hope this flight will last

But no, all fun things come to an end
This flying thingy slows
The doors open, I'm in your arms
New sensations for my nose

Ok I got it now
I'm supposed to walk with you
But I'd rather that you carry me
Because so many things are new

Of course I had to stop and sniff
And I really had to pee
So I did because
It is one thing puppy's do you see

All the way encouraged
I seem to do no wrong
Because you know I'm learning
With you I can be strong

That's what best friends do
They encourage and understand
They build each other up
And they're always paw in hand

So if you are like I am
And everything seems new
Trust your friend to be there
And always walk with you

So I'm Maisey pup dog
I'm still quite small
But you really seem to love me
With my furry toes and all

You accept who I am
And I accept you
Puppies are like children in ways
But we have 4 legs and you have 2

New home to roam
New senses to sense
Smells, sights and sounds
You and I, for each other we are meant

Here it comes, my first horror
I have to share my new space and friend
With two furry, meowing things
I hope these new things end

I am 5 years old today
My bestie told me that
I still remember when we met
Especially your silly hat

So these are thing I know that I know
I can't pee or poo on the floor
I shouldn't bark to loud
But I can certainly scratch at the door

I know all of my toys by name
I especially love my ball
Because when you throw I fetch
It's give and take for all

I know I don't like cats much
But I really know you do
So these things I accept
Just to be with you

We still go in the flying car
I've learned it's color is black
But I'm always close to you
Even though I sit in the back

It's always ok to take a back seat
It's ok to be seen and heard
But the most amazing thing I've learned
Is that love can be shared without words

I hope you like these words I write
It's hard to type with paws
Sometimes I hit the wrong button
But I can always pause

Correct, make it right
I'm not perfect at all
But I hope you keep me with you
WITH MY FURRY TOES AND ALL

Your best friend Maisey May Dog

PS
If you like me and want to know more
I am an Aussie Shepherd
Three colors in fact
I even smile, and know some words

Printed in the United States
By Bookmasters